KEROSENE

KEROSENE

Jamella Hagen

NIGHTWOOD EDITIONS

Nightwood Editions
P.O. Box 1779
Gibsons, BC von 1vo
Canada
www.nightwoodeditions.com

Cover design by Anna Comfort
Printed and bound in Canada on 100% post-consumer recycled, ancient-forest-
free paper, processed chlorine-free and printed with vegetable-based dyes.

Nightwood Editions acknowledges financial support from the Government
of Canada through the Canada Book Fund and the Canada Council for
the Arts, and from the Province of British Columbia through the British
Columbia Arts Council and the Book Publisher's Tax Credit.

Library and Archives Canada Cataloguing in Publication

Hagen, Jamella, 1980–
    Kerosene / Jamella Hagen.

Poems.
ISBN 978-0-88971-263-8

    I. Title.

PS8615.A363K47 2011   C811'.6   C2011-904674-1

CONTENTS

III.

I.

Linguistics

First: a bird feeder, through the glass. There was no
electricity, I was one when the ram
knocked me unconscious. Saws at the small mill
hummed a comfort in the distance; a flowering
of peas swung heavy on the netting. Seconds
passed and then a blue slit of sky.
Opened. Gust of rough cotton
verbing the afternoon back down.

According to my mother, when asked
what happened, all I could say was *bird*.

An Introduction to My Mother

Scene 1: Bathtub

She's standing naked
in the bathtub at midnight, in her gumboots.
Beneath her feet, the submerged
pack rat trap: long wood box
with a trick door. Inside it, the rat
drowning. My brother sleeping upstairs.

Night ticks forward quiet as a child's
held breath, the light switched off, water
flat as a mirror—until the rat
untricks the hatch and springs out,
wet and mad and desperate.

Did they look each other in the eye
before she started stomping?

Scene 2: Semi-Automatic

Her father wouldn't spend that money
on college, but after she left California
for Canada, took root in the bush
and had two babies, he bought her rifles
in case of bear attack.

Each time we visited, he sent her home
with another gun. At the San Jose airport

after he gave her the .30-06 for Christmas,
she wrestled a cart, both children,
that long grey case. The pile beginning
to shift. *Mom, mom, the gun's falling,*
I called out as we approached the security lineup.

Scene 3: Broken Windows

As far as I know, she only ever used the guns
inside the house. First a pack rat,
which she shot along with the window
of the back room. That splintered mouth
gaped for years until she could afford
to replace the glass. Next the Saturday morning tomcat,
shot from her bedroom window at 6 am,
rocketing my brother and me from sleep.
But when the bears came, lunging slick
and drenched from the river, pushing their damp
black noses out of the bush and ambling
through the yard, she left the bullets
on that high shelf in her bedroom
and let them pass.

Scene 4: Hands

Broken hatchets, hand-me-down
chainsaws. Washing her hair. Milking, spinning
sheep's wool into sweaters. Pouring sugar
and cream over the raspberries.

My Father Explains

That first winter
your mother and I had goats—
we lived upstairs in the bedroom
the goats lived downstairs,
that's why there are tooth marks
all over the living room walls.

We butchered once a year.
Afterward, I couldn't eat meat for weeks
but your mother
would run back, throw the bleeding livers
into the pan and eat them. You know,
you were always like your mother that way,
always liked liver.

Dragging the Cabin

It would be easier, they thought,
to move the six-sided cabin they'd built
than to start again with a pile
of logs, spikes and two-by-fours, so

my parents unroofed the place shingle
by shingle to avoid snagging
passing hydro wires, pried out all the glass
windows, jacked up the walls and floor,

the wood cookstove still inside,
loaded the thing on skids and dragged it
eight miles on gravel roads. Needless
to say, the skids—two huge spruce—

shredded beneath it as they hauled.
The logs began to shift, unhinging
at each of the six corners
and the floor beneath the cookstove

splintered, heaved, gave itself up
to the rutted driveway, that long dirt
track thick with timothy, chickweed,
the occasional lowbush blueberry.

Break on Through

My father's been married three times but never
to my mother. And though they're both
from the geranium suburbs of California
they've never seen each other there
except in photographs. After holidays south
of the border one or the other would ask me:
*Did your dad take you to the beach? Did your mother
show you the small world or the teacup ride?*

My mother left him before I could walk.
Creating baseball board games in the hexagonal
house he built and rebuilt to his own
evolving design. Tending the rain barrels.
He never did get used to the cold—he'd crawl
cursing under the stuck truck to fasten the chains,
growl as the wheelbarrow slipped and scraped
on a rubble of ice.

Those early days he worked sorting ore
at Baker Mine, reliving his time
at UCLA delivering pharmaceuticals
to the stars, watching the Doors play live
at the Whisky a Go Go. At parties he'd gesture
to the flaking face of Jim Morrison
on his favourite blue sweatshirt and reminisce:

I said to Robby Kreiger, the guitarist, 'Hey,
you guys are going to be great, you're going
to be famous,' and he said, 'Thanks, I sure
hope you're right.'

He started writing a music column
for the local newspapers. The green mailbox
at the end of the road overflowed with vinyl,
cassettes, CDs. He filled the shelves,
thumbtacked them to the walls: Lou
Reed washed in blue, Patti Smith
in her white nightgown, Laurie Anderson
with a light bulb in her mouth.

Outside, the lawn was a hayfield
he cut with a scythe. All that brome
and fescue. The war he'd eluded
blooming like a jungle
as he swept the blade—shh, shh
through the pale green stalks.

Kerosene

What we used to burn for light
before power lines snapped and hummed
their way down the hill, pushing
thin-skinned poplars to the ground.

Next came propane, fat globe lamps
that lit with a soft whump, drew
bugs to their fragile wicks, which
crumbled to ash if you touched them

and you did, being younger, being a boy.
You threatened to hit me with firewood,
did with that yellow plastic pole
I used to play horse-jump in the front yard.

Half-siblings, we sparred with fingernails
and baby teeth, bows and arrows
and GT Snow Racers. I still see you
headed down the icy driveway toward

that tree at the corner. Now you're working
for the university, living on a maple-lined
street in Vancouver. Life's a beach, you say,
though someone is stealing your mail.

Do you ever turn back, dredge up
the radio phone, the root cellar, the day

a mother bear huffed on your shoes
and trapped you in that tree for hours

at the top of the drive? Or are you all eyes
forward, hair flying back, wind whipping
at your frost-bitten ears, happy enough
to be sliding somewhere fast?

Early Life on the Farm

Still, at night, I wake up
to a clatter of hooves, crush
of tin-can claustrophobia, a dark
and scrabbling thing—for months
afterward I called every shadow *pig*.
How did they butcher them?
I only recall the body strung
from a tractor, the empty crate.
I asked, *Will they butcher*
the rest of us? and refused
to climb upstairs through the trap door
in the ceiling. Now, the details
worn thin, simply that
darkness, that squeeze.

Suskwa

Meltwater just down
from the mountains, thigh deep
and so fast we used two gnarled sticks
to help us cross, our feet bruising
as they slipped on shifting rocks. Naked
as young animals, we made it through
to the other side, to the beaver ponds
where we balanced on wet logs and swam
until our lips were the colour of saskatoons.
On the way back, muscles
awkward from the cold, we laughed
because we couldn't speak, because we
didn't need to, bushwhacked back
to our clothes, which we could hardly
put on, then shivered our way
up the trail to stand wringing our hair
by the hot wood stove, telling it
to the grown-ups, waiting
for the beans to warm so we could eat
even though we'd been eating all day,
soapberries, old man's beard, other
lichens—things we claimed to love
because we'd found them ourselves.

Fall

This quiet disaster
of thirteen, a split
caught somewhere between the ends
of my hair and the frayed beginnings
of my low-slung jeans.
You could say I fell
from a horse, and where
he touched me

the day the ground dragged
the wind down to it and my
back neck face breasts belly and—

then nothing
but breathless brown grass, dirt
in my teeth and the horse,
still running.

It would be two years
till I could sit again. I stretched my body flat
as a ripped page, watched
the sun slide a lazy palm
across the days. The nights were cold
but warmer than they could have been.
It wasn't all accident. I adjusted the helmet
and jumped.

Driving Daytona

They called it *Daytona*, driving the same loop
    through town, over and over in Jeff's white van
with the rusted rear fenders and dirty carpeted interior
    the same musty shade of brown as every cheap
motel. There were three Hazeltons—Old Town, New
    Town and South Town—Daytona was mostly
old and new, they'd turn up the music
    and you'd lie down in the back of the van
with the other girls. Cannibal Corpse, Deicide,
    Sepultura, the boys kept joking
they'd start their own Northern BC metal band
    called Chainsawdomy. Shane wore a black T-shirt
every day that read *Butchered at Birth* with an image
    of bleeding skeletons lifting bleeding fetuses
from bleeding rib cages. You loved those boys,
    in your own way. Watched them try
to break beer bottles over their heads one
    after another. The bottles never broke and neither
did the picnic table they threw into the lake or
    the mood that settled in the morning after,
Shane hanging limp out the window,
    the van dragging heavy through gravel,
through queasy stands of poplar and cottonwood,
    hauling its sad sick cargo back to town.

After the Moon's Gone Down

1.

Why is it when you're lonely you remember
        being alone? Or when you're stoned
all the memories of being stoned
        come flooding back? Suddenly,
you're lonely and stoned and sixteen
        wandering the dark with a boy
you hardly know, red willows brushing
        at your cheeks like hands, sounds
of a distant crowd sifting clear
        as church bells through the whip-red
branches.

2.

And you're stumbling toward the outhouse,
        vomiting across the path. The girls
at the fire suck back Kahlúa Mudslides and laugh
        as you fall into a bush of ripe thimbleberries,
swear you won't hotknife anymore—you can
        still feel the burn in your throat, hot
sandpaper, the way you sucked it in and held,
        having watched grown-ups do it all your life.

You sprawl. You sprawl in the gravel and thimbleberries
        in the yarrow and stinging nettles and if you move
your face you'll be sick so you hold on
        with your whole body, to this ground, this mud,
this little hill above Pentz Lake while bone by bone
        the chill seeps in, and you sleep.

3.

Marley holds the jar in his hands, says the peaches
        taste like tomatoes, and they do. You eat them
anyway. Also, a tray full of french fries
        a half-pan of chocolate brownies
and a bowlful of instant noodle soup. You like
        that you can eat as much as they can
and sometimes more. You like it when
        they're afraid of the bush in the dark.
You like them standing clumped by the fire
        with glowing amber bottles in their hands.
You hate them too. You hate them shit-kicking
        in cowboy boots, you hate the snuff container
rings on the back pockets of their jeans, you hate
        the ones who hate you for being smart
at school, for being skinny, for being uncool
        and you'll only take your pants off for boys
from out of town, only
        swim naked after the moon's gone
down.

Girls' Wrestling Team

Blue rush of spandex against our cheeks,
the stick and skid of boots against
rubber, the pause, shift and torque,
spin of a hinge coming loose

    ankle pick.

We trained in the grey basement, loose fibreglass
sifted in tiny itching filaments from the ceiling
as we somersaulted, somersaulted
in our stone-hued sweatsuits

        hip-toss.

The lot of us sitting in chemistry class, passing
words for food: peaches, linguini, tin-roof
ice cream. The body will crave anything
it can't have; we wanted to eat things

half-nelson

we didn't even like. Lean animals
at the end of winter we gnawed toward
weigh-ins, boiled one single egg each
and drove half-dizzy to the dance

shoulder throw

where Kate lifted a six-foot speaker
single-handed and charmed the deejays.
Summers, we fundraised in clear-cuts,
hoisting half-burnt hemlock into pickups

fireman's carry

to sell for stove wood. Wanting those
sixteen-hour journeys to the south
in unmarked rental vans, wanting
to bruise, push, tease, drag, haul our way

double-leg takedown

some place new.

Fieldmice

They've been there all along. Tunnels
in spring, their bottom halves
lying like highways over the fields
after the snow has melted. You don't see
the mice—they've gone deeper now,
under the long grass—but you imagine
that heavy white ceiling, whiskers
pressed back, a cold scurrying.
And you find out your best friend's mother
is dying of cancer and you are going to leave this place,
like your heart, behind, and your father will move to Hawaii
taking nothing but his good shoes,
and the field will grow up with spruce trees
tall as chimneys, lonely as clocktowers. The mice
will still be there. In winter, a metropolis of little feet
travelling in blind tunnels under the snow.

II.

View from the Hammock

Monkeys love the pitanga
bush, they're always in there,
stroking the red berries.

Babies slung around their necks
soft as peaches, small as squirrels,
tufts of hair protruding from their ears.

If you reach out your hand, they'll
reach back.

Leaving the North

I was known there for falling
from horses, hillsides, the tops of poplars
that didn't bend as expected but

snapped. I left that place
pulling burrs from my hair, nursing
scraped knees and a bad

habit of wandering alone
after dark. Wound up in this city
with four white walls and no way

to read them, streets dusky and
swarming, a little Plato,
a little Hobbes to fill up

the loneliness. Sports cars droned
past the windows and short,
brutish shadows slid like hands

up the walls of the cave. I went
to parties, evading sleep
and reason as long as I could,

which was a long time. Eventually
came down with a cough
I couldn't shake, got the feeling

that in this city if you split open
any wall, you'd find
something awful inside—

mould, asbestos, parts
of lost women. So many
were missing then. It was a record year

for rain. Water was a door
we went through each morning
and emerged from each night,

amphibious.

Signs of Things to Come

I was playing flag football, mud-shirred
and breathless, you brought
cinnamon buns from the Alma Street bakery,
a flock of geese lifted their wet feet
from the mud and edged themselves
into the wind.

Soft click of the lock in our rented
hilltop apartment as we
moved in together, finished university.
You drove tours along the bear-strewn
highways; I taught *she might, he could, they
should*, in a light-locked classroom
downtown. Red velour slipped daily
off the smooth shoulders of the sofa,
every window faced the North Shore,
its legions of nimbus.

I read Mallory, and the horses
shook the floor with their hooves.
Percival's sister gave herself up
in the kitchen; they set her in a ship, sailed it
toward the grail on a wave of rain
that looked like the sea.

One afternoon you pushed your fist
through the Gyproc
where the rain had softened it.
A little exit. We sold our clocks and
radios, booked two tickets to Peru.

Scenes from Bus Windows (Lima to Huaraz, Peru)

White columns of Lima give way
to hillsides of mud brick shacks,
sudden scorch of desert,
a military base marked by a tank
on duty, a banner advertising Pepsi.

Higher up in the hills when the windows
fog over, I use my hand to clear
a little view into the rain. Goats
tethered outside small wet houses
remind me of home.

Cordillera Huayhuash

The tent walls tight
above us, thin and veined
as leaves, light sinking slowly
outside, the lake quiet,
all the small splashing fish
fed and gone under,

the lightning takes us
by surprise—a flare against the pale
green ceiling. We curl our bodies
around each other, sleeping bags
softening our sharp edges, the day's
disagreements, how we turned
separately around a boulder in the scree,
lost each other for hours. Now
we listen to the hoarse roar
of thunder, and the avalanches
coming down and down
throughout the night.

In the morning, the air gone clear again,
white trails mark the slopes
of the mountains—so narrow,
so slight, we might not have noticed them
except for the memory of rumbling
snow, your breath in my hair,
the way you reached your hand

out of the sleeping bag,
unzipped the door to let the wind
gust in off the glaciers.

Scenes from Bus Windows (La Paz to Cochabamba, Bolivia)

Two trucks overturned and burning
on the highway, behind them two, maybe three
hundred arms linked in protest. Tires, couches,
old shoes—they've blocked the road with anything,
set the barricade on fire.

We've got one choice: fork left
where the road's still clear, leave them
their piles of rage, burning phrases.

Is this what we wanted, stories
of risk and revolt, the moment gone taut
as the bus slows, as passengers
shout and stand, as we sit silent as pig-children,
noses to the glass?

Salar de Uyuni

This salt. Wide white table
of prairie four thousand metres
above the sea. We drive for hours to reach
the edge, find water skinned over
with ice or boiling out of the mud. Four days
in a Jeep without heat, who cares
what the temperature is. Flamingos
don't give it a number, just keep breaking
through the ice until they can't
break through anymore. Hot pink
flutter of wings in the dry blue air.

At night we drink tequila, toss dice
from a leather *cacho* cup, bury ourselves
under layers of llama blankets, the weight of them
pressing us to sleep. Not much
to burn here, the hotels cold
as Christmas—water in the toilet
freezes in the night. Nearby geysers
spew steam into the air—warm,
treacherous, undrinkable. Next stop
a three-day fiesta in a town where small boys
lead drunken grandmothers through
the narrow dark streets.

It's brand new—the old town bought up
by Canadian miners, then moved five
kilometres across the Altiplano. Houses
are bare plywood with bedrooms
the temperature of hockey arenas.
People wind scarves around their throats
to cook breakfast, then tunnel under
the ghosted streets for profit that leaves,
like the tourists, on the afternoon train.

Last day on this desert plateau, we stop
at a railway graveyard scrawled
with graffiti: *Así es la vida. Se necesita*
un mecanico con experiencia. There are no
tracks; we climb the rusted
engines as though they were horses,
aim ourselves toward the static horizon.

Road to Viração, Northeast Brazil

Some days, I take the Fusca.
Pale as butter, it melts in the sun.

Other days, I ride the blue schoolbus
unless it's late, having hit a cow.

Then, I walk fast with a black umbrella
to keep off the midday heat. Once a man

with a motorcycle offered a ride. I slipped
in the dust, seared my calf on the muffler;

it burned for an hour. The Canadian-Brazilians
laughed. *Maria Gasolina*, they said. *That was not*

your boyfriend's muffler. So I avoid
motorbikes, squeeze into farm trucks

full of silent, sweaty men on their way
from the field. When I arrive at the school

I unlock it, teach my class. *Present perfect*, I say
is for the past whose location in time is

irrelevant. Say you've spit watermelon seeds off
the porch and they've grown into vines. What do you care

when the seed started growing, so long as
you can eat the fruit now?

Eclipse

That night we tucked chillies inside potatoes,
tinfoiled and cooked them in the fire.

Roasted corn cobs and biscuit dough
twisted around sticks as we waited. Discovering

the way old bamboo explodes in the fire,
each chamber bursting. The way the tongue

finds a buried chilli, all around it
a slow burn. The way an eclipse of the moon

moves slowly, until suddenly, the dark
hems you in. Afterward, we walked back

to our cabin under the jackfruit tree, dug into
our pockets, discovered we'd lost

our skeleton key. We had to break in,
crawling over the wall and squeezing

through the ventilation space under
the roof tiles, then slept uneasily, something

about that locked blue door. In the morning,
when we slithered back out, searched the rock

where the fire had been, spread the coals
across the ground, we found the key

melted: a solid metal pool.

Scenes from Bus Windows
(Puerto Madryn to Rio Gallegos, Argentina)

The only constant is the wind. Sunsets
last for an hour, the sky hums pink
against the glass.

Tangled in a barbed wire fence,
the skeleton of a rearing guanaco,
head thrown back, mouth open
to the wide blue dome.

Perito Moreno

Ice. The long white tongue of it.
All day this glacier
breaks

and falls thundering, piece
by piece, into the blue.
Icebergs bob in the swells, one

turns over—slow tilt, then a quick slip
and burst of submerged ice. Naked,
wet-blue, it drifts loose of this

sixty-metre wall of evidence things are
slipping away. Each time
a piece calves off, the lake rises

to receive it. A wave ripples out
and sweeps the shore, collecting
what it can. Travellers

have disappeared this way,
washed under in their quest
to get close, to get closer.

Questions of Travel

–After Elizabeth Bishop

1.

On the steel walkway that spans the waterfall,
the yawning *Garganta del Diablo*, you lose your hat
to a sudden wet gust; watch it sail like a flimsy
cotton ship into the rolling kettle of the falls.
You watch it go. That roaring will stick to your ribs
like grilled *lomo fino*, years later you'll still hear it
in airports and subway stations,
feel the steel girders shudder under your feet.
You learn to fall asleep anywhere
except your own bed. Sometimes
you wake up with bumps on your head
where it has knocked into the window of a bus,
or the welded passenger cage on the back
of a converted pickup.

2.

And why the attraction
in the first place? As though it's all better
than the people, places, possibilities
you already know. So you can come fresh
at all the things you hate about
yourself—your awkwardness at dinner parties,
karaoke, small town postal outlets.
The questions, *¿De dónde eres? ¿De qué país?*

other versions of why are you here
and where's your wedding ring,
your offspring, your sense of purpose
and community.

3.

But then, wouldn't it have been a shame not
to have sat in the road playing cards next
to that dead dog thinking it alive,
really, not to have watched the driver fixing
the differential with a kitchen knife,
not to have ascended that road on bald tires,
in the snow, praying with all your atheist soul
to a distant plaster statue of the Virgin Mary.
Not to have had your disposable camera stolen
by a girl named Soledad whom you befriended
on a bus. And not to have spent that night in the ruins
in a tent surrounded by dogs, and in the morning
when you woke up on the dewless cement slab
to have been offered a personalized tour where, for the first time,
you could follow whole sentences in Spanish. Not to have heard
those Brazilian campaign songs blasted from the backs
of transport trucks, pickups, bicycles, so loud
you had to shut your mouth and let them shake you.
And never to have smelled these hectic streets,
this soup that first made you turn away,
but now makes you want nothing
more than to be here, now, in this restaurant,
filling yourself with it.

Scenes from Bus Windows (Santiago to Arica, Chile)

The ocean, the Atacama, sky the colour
of a faded blue dress as though the sand
has scrubbed the colour out. We pass a truckload
of toilets smashed on the roadside, a bloated cow
in the dunes, four legs stuck straight out, balloon cow.
To Arica, the border zone, where Chile swallowed
Bolivia's access to the sea, pushed back
Peru. Everywhere barbed wire and Coca-Cola
signs: *Coca-Cola, Bienvenido a Arica; Coca-Cola*
Terminal de Omnibus; then a Coca-Cola playground,
its swings and seesaws painted white and red;
the hillsides scarred with graffiti, *Pedro*
te amo, and there again in perfect, lover's scrawl
Coca-Cola. We take a taxi along the two-lane
highway to the border, minefields on either side.
A sign reads: *Cuida tu vida, abrocha el cinturon*
de seguridad, but we have no seatbelts—even
the driver has only half, which he pulls across his lap
hopeful as an unclasped hand. He crosses himself
each time we pass a roadside shrine. Not much
farther now, and it's hard to believe it won't
be like this always, this chugging forward, this metal
and glass, this improvised formula
for getting by, getting past.

III.

Portrait of a City

Bicycles and smokestacks. Red cranes of the shipyard. Piles of sulphur, yellow as sunlight. Spinal arch of the Lions Gate emerging from the fog. Bookstores and bistros. Your favourite chocolate shop, a chili in each steaming mug. The towers where you slept and studied with views every night of sunsets over the bay. You took hundreds of pictures, imitating Gertrude Stein who said every repetition is different from the one before. On the day of the earthquake, Lear on the heath and the room swung forward on its pillars, the towers swayed above the ocean, and the sand beneath the university shifted like sugar in a bowl that is rocked back and forth by a child.

Tuesday Morning

Nausea a wave to ride on, a dizzy
rocking. Picture something hollow:
a skull blown clean by the wind, a door
left open in the rain. Wait, that's not right.

I was reading a poem about carpentry
when the woman downstairs rang to tell me
hot water was pouring down her wall.
We tucked our heads under my sink,
listened to the rushing. Pressed our hands
against the hot wallpaper, felt it swell
under our fingers.

The plumber bored through the cabinet
then went at the bedroom wall.
From two feet away, you could feel
the heat coming off it. He sawed open
that hot wet mess inside, worked it
with his fingers, resealed the hissing pipes,
swept up the drywall but left the hole
gaping open, the apartment a damp sauna.

Nothing changed, except
I wasn't nauseous anymore, only hungry
squeezed by that fear, still with me
after all these years, of having made
a mistake, of preparing
to pay for it.

Field Trip

I take my ESL public speaking students
to the Law Courts for their afternoon
elective. Slick with salt-mist, the grey
cement of it is nearly invisible
on this wet afternoon
but we locate an unlocked door.
The defendant does not recall
taking the crowbar to the gas station, trouble
with the attendant—thrown back
into a wall of Cheetos and chocolates,
money and the idea of money
spilling from his jeans as he spins,
rushes the back door, the getaway car, leaves
the crowbar on the counter, a wet smear
of tires in the empty asphalt lot.

When I look, every one of my students
has fallen asleep. *The lawyers
spoke too quickly*, they say. *We couldn't
understand anything they said.*

Bicycle

Warm morning after rain, steaming streets
slowly serpentine, I buy a bicycle
from the used shop on Dunbar where the price
reflects its fluorescent momentum

and I expect then, to neglect it, to overlook
its lean steel frame and chase four-wheeled
alternatives, but in a red hooded jacket
find myself riding even when November

sets in to sluice this city of its confusions.
Quiet and spin, flush and burn, the climb
to the huge green lawn at the park overlooking
a string of sand stitched to the city lights

and there was that evening of leaves
resting like eyelashes across the streets
and as I rode by in the dark
someone called out to me from a doorway

There's a new president!

Girls' Wrestling Team (2)

The night Carol takes to the mat
in Beijing, 2 am Pacific Time,
flicker of a borrowed television set
against a darkened window,
rain outside hitting the Vancouver
street like the tip-tap of a nervous
heartbeat, the patter and rush
of an Olympic takedown. Gold

a colour we carry in myth and
whispers, under our tongues, like the story
of the fair unknown who arrives
to unseat the expected. As if we bit down, felt
it give, cathartic, beneath an incisor.

Carol steps forward
in her red and white
and I remember her saying
that there are so many ways
to win or lose a match
leverage or surprise or attrition etcetera
and I have watched her system
of slow and relentless advance,
quick points to an offset rhythm as the seconds
tick down. This time, for the first time

in the stands: a father, a sister,
a television camera panning in
for the final arm-raise.

What I Think of When My Father Calls

The time we visited the couple in California who kept an owl called Archimedes and a unicorn goat. The owl perched in the living room, folding and unfolding his wings above newspapers scattered over the hardwood. The unicorn's name I forget, but I remember the woman describing how when the goat was born, she surgically opened his forehead and twisted the horns, which had not yet surfaced, so they grew into one long straight lance. It looked just like in pictures. The goat was white and shaggy and disappointing to me since I was seven and wanted unicorns to be horses. *Oh no,* she assured me, *they've always been goats, historically.* And on the long trip home, I had this dream about Ronald Reagan, who all the adults were talking about then: there were people riding on unicorn goats to be near him, they were riding down a hill and crossing a large highway, which was their test, because the highway was filled with hurrying cars. It stretched all the way to the border with Canada.

Still

What it looks like, on the kitchen table, with its glass jugs and carbon:
one part animal, one part old-fashioned doctor's office,

everything boiled in water and set out ready. She does not take
a photograph. To do so may be incriminating. She does, however,

have a taste—mixed with orange juice and a splash of Five Alive,
the glass clear as a lens. Through it she can see her bicep, the sleeve

of her red shirt, belted at the waist in the new style. *Well, aren't you
gussied up*, her brother says, though it's Christmas Eve

and even in this town, that means something. The spruce lit up
in the corner, giving off a tang. Deaths in her family

have looked like this. Sugared. Distilled.
Now the brother is putting on

Sinatra, the logs are giving off heat
they've been holding all day. Does she consider herself

to be on loan from the metropolis? Moonshine
should cure that, and the pretty, silted snowflakes

puddling onto the floor beside her shoes.

Queen of the North

1.

I remember
rocking, slap-slapping, waves
against hull, waves
against the wall next to
                        the bed. Against
my ear, pressed
        to the inside shipwall. Dark wood,
weathered. Like docks, like
        the dock we walked along
to visit his house, the house
                        he built
with his ship-weathered hands. Those walls
        white as milk, white
as new teeth. Ceiling a raft
                of cedar, floor
a slick sea of pine. Beams thick
        as torsos, beams holding up
those walls. That spiral staircase.

2.

I was in Korea when the news
came through,
hunched over a desk stacked with English.
The *Queen of the North*

                    sunk.
Two passengers lost at sea.
Something in my throat shifted,
listed. *I've taken
that ferry*, I said.

We slept below sea level. My mother,
      my brother and I. There's a photograph
of me on deck in a plastic chair, thirteen
         in my cherry-red sweatshirt, hair
blown tangled across my eyes.

3.

Later, a name
    on the evening news. The officer
on the bridge, navigating. I'd been to his house, the house
      he built with his own
hammers and chisels,
    it had windows looking out on
      the sea. Every detail
a carving. Door handles, banisters, edges of roofs.
In the garden,
flowers as tall as your head, stone pathways
to get lost in. At least that's the way
    I remember it.

Slap-slapping. Press of waves
    moving forward toward
a mouth, a channel, the broad hips
      of an island. Rumour. We
hold our breath, sink into it. It muffles
the sounds in our ears.

Each Green Signpost

Time measured in a horizon of dead pines.
Some years gone, and this little pickup, lightly rusted,
four cylinders to send me through
these hills of low-bellied cows, packed earth
under patent wheels of Fords, fields creased
like old denim in the brief heat
of July and a beneath it all, a low
rumble of insects chewing their way
eastward.

I have a friend who fights fires, she
soaks the scorched earth and emerges
sooted, singed at the hem, says,
This isn't California, sometimes we let
the doomed suburbs burn but—
Still. Beetles leave their ascomycetes,
their blue stain, winter
slips her feet a little further up the map.

This tinder keeps on blooming.
We're struck like lodgepoles
in a storm empty of rain
in this matchbook forest that
blazed gold and dried standing.

Matters of Scale

I know a boy who makes fish lures,
trouble follows him everywhere.
In dreams sockeye spill
loose change and cocaine
but he loves that silted river.
If you saw where he came from
you'd glimpse what intervenes—
biologists say these forests
all grow from the bodies
of fish dragged by wing
or by jaw across every finned
and saw-toothed mountain range.

When I was ten, and tasked with
throwing the rotting carcasses of pinks
hauled up by the dog back
into the heaving waves of the Bulkley,
I remember how easily they split open
at the touch of a gloved hand and from their
silver skin spilt a liquid
already squirming with new life.

Presently, an upstream struggle
for fewer fish, coal beds
at the headwaters and farmed Atlantics
at the mouth, fish guides resisting

the distant calls of Alberta, but in August
those rivers are glacial green
and steelhead still ply the slipstreams.

Questions of Home

On s'habitue à tout

—*Camus*

1.

My mother's two-room cabin of black
particleboard, bramble of red
osier dogwood and devil's club, a fast and
glacial river where a woman once
went under.

They say she drowned the year
frost killed all the green beans
in the middle of July. She washed up
under the bridge like all
the bodies do, a strong swimmer only
her arms had been zipped inside her jacket,
the sleeves left empty.

My mother told me the story, gesturing
across the lawn toward the rock outcrop
where the currents cut close, saying, *That's where
they think she went in.* I sifted
through long insomniac evenings, waiting
for a sign, though of course
she never came.

2.

This hotel room. This porcelain
and plastic, this painted sailboat
and singed grey sea. The way notions
of home overlap each other,
like fine layers of shale. If you crack
the whole thing with a hammer,
the pieces come loose
in your hands.

3.

The cool floor of a dank apartment
in Honolulu. The dim back bedroom
of a low stucco home in San Jose. Bunk
bed in Salta with a blue duvet. The cab
of a rusting pickup truck parked in a field,
the windshield long smashed in,
where two teenage boys blow smoke
into each other's mouths.

Anywhere can feel like home
if you lie there long enough
staring at the ceiling.

Emma and Rosemary

1: Emma

Emma had red hair in two braids
when I had only wayward blonde tufts.
An early memory: we are two,
Emma makes me a mud pie
and I eat it. Just before Christmas
she tells me to climb the high shelf
and hand down the gifts, wrapped
and sealed with Scotch Tape, so I do and she
unwraps all of them. We are
the best of friends. Emma
prefers the icing and I will eat
nothing but the cake itself.

2: Rosemary

Willow catkins in spring
remind me of Rosemary
who would dredge the snow swamps
of February to collect them
each year, religiously. Found objects
were important to her, animate
and inanimate both: stones
pulled from the Kispiox,
perfectly symmetrical spruce
for the holidays, a small orange
kitten trundling the roadside dust.

3: Foothills

When Emma and I are teenagers
and Rosemary is dying
in the blue recliner by the unfinished
spiral staircase, she takes photographs
of us standing beside the tall cactus.
Emma is taller even than the cactus,
she is wearing a shirt from Le Château
with *Sexy Love* scripted in silver
across the breasts. Rosemary
complains bitterly about the shirt,
shoots the ironic smile of a mother's
distress toward the blue velour.
Emma calls out to the cats through the open
sliding glass door.

4: Distance

The year we graduate, Rosemary
gives me two things. First, a plastic
toolbox from Lee Valley containing
scissors, utility razor blades and a blue
crowbar. Then, when I leave town
she who has no spare cash to speak of
sends a parcel of rocks through the mail.
The note reads: *To keep you grounded
in the big city.* I call Emma from my new
cordless phone. She asks if it's raining
and I ask the same. That was the first year

we knew the weather was different because
no snow fell—even for Emma—until January.

5: *Thaw*

Emma is married in February. Bridesmaid,
I wear open-toed shoes
into the snow for pictures. We
hold the smiles of twenty below
for too long and afterward run our feet
under hot water to warm them.
Rosemary is a silence that everyone
hears; there is a vase
of budding willows set by the long table.
After the ceremony, fireworks
shoot through the parking lot and break
in slow showers across the hill.

6: *New*

This April morning, time has gone sideways,
for Emma, after two sleepless nights and a pain
that surges and recedes like surf
against a spring shore. When the time comes,
and does not come, and comes to surgery,
the anaesthetist tells me, *Look if you want,*
look away if you want. If you feel dizzy,
put your head between your knees.
I look of course though later couldn't tell you
precisely what took place or

the identity of anyone in the room save
myself, Emma (eyelids fluttering) and
when he comes, the red-haired infant who turns
so suddenly toward the sound of her voice.

7: Willows . . .

are the last trees to fully leaf out in spring
and the earliest yellow in August
when the first pomegranate breath
of rain goes sifting over
the tinder hayfields. They have a voracious
thirst; in a yard the roots run deep,
brushing the cheek of the underworld,
splitting pipes if they can to siphon
the spill of your tap. It can seem
unjust, as a thief who sips fuel in the night
from a tank you were certain
had miles left to burn. Only in the
seeping ice of winter's end will they
extend a bouquet of small gestures
soft as earlobes, pale as moons,
which shock once against the sudden bare skin
of your hand on a melting afternoon
and are gone.

Hush and Thrum

Highway 37 North, a road blown clean
of expectation. This new turn
toward polarity, revolving axis
of so much equatorial spin. It's enough:
plate glass and plastic, a warm motor
to spark a course through this post-
Christmas hush and thrum.

In Meziadin, snow whips in
thick as cream. A dim noon
carries me past the yellow hulks
of ploughs, buried loaves of spruce.
The moon, when it comes, looms round
as a sugar cookie in the glazed
fly-wing iridescence of the sky.

Crossing to the drifted parking lot
of the diner, frost thickens
my eyelashes. Inside, the sandwich
is open faced, rich with gravy,
the walls hung with strange cautions:
photographs of wrecked semis,
snarled steel twisted in an arctic wind.
I wish a steady hand on the moustached
truckers in the window seat, their
idling rigs and necessary cargo.

Back on the vaulted highway,
headlights shore a small forest,
the cold creates its own hunger
to continue. Even in the dark, you can see
where the tufted hooves of caribou
have sifted into the snowbanks
in search of food.

Sleeper

Enjoying the moment of liftoff
as when the airplane of the soul leaves
the tarmac of the body. The voice
in the radio tower
forever giving the *all clear*.
Imagine from the vantage of
that tower, all the sleepers rising up
each night through a scrim
of low cloud. And what murmurings
might go said or unsaid on those
airwaves. I spend every Friday night
at the beer-steeped curling rink
with the air traffic controllers
of the only major airport in this country
still without radar. They bring in
the planes with binoculars, and by
the voice of each pilot, which they know nearly
by heart. They are skilled curlers,
each stone travels down the pebbled
ice like a Boeing 757
coming in for taxi. Precision
is a skill linked to the stratosphere, sleep
its uncanny double. I've never been a good shot
in any sport and I'll take liftoff
over landing any day, but sometimes
I catch sunrise over the curving rim
of the earth from an airplane window,
beckoning all its slumberers back down.

Crossings

1.

Impossible to cut a horse loose
from its history. Take, for example,
this farm I know

where the old Percheron and his life partner,
a half-draft chestnut, slipped through
the open gate one day,

turned up weeks later
muzzling the slatted fence
outside the field where

they'd been born some thirty
years before and sixty kilometres
away. Their route finding was remarkable

but even more so
their crossing of a certain bridge
spanning a canyon, one hoof

in front of the other, the bridge deck
ringing out underfoot as they picked
their way over, one hundred metres

above the river. Did they cross in the dark,
when even horses, unseeing, can navigate
an open steel grating suspended in the air?

2.

Amber liquid in a bowl,
I light the wick carefully,
set the glass chimney

in place. Rest a hand
against the glass, take up
a little heat.

All night, the lamp smokes
imperceptibly. The walls won't
show it yet for years, but

if a hand passes
above the flame, it draws
a sooty line across the skin.

3.

Beside the new bridge, ghost
of the old: cement pilings, cable anchor points
where the colonial cart bridge used to be. Further,
a worn rock where, earlier still, a footbridge
ran suspended by ropes between the cleft
stone walls, swinging perpetually in the updrafts.

4.

Third beach, Vancouver: we watch
police officers ride their horses
into the ocean. The animals
snort and stamp, they toss

their heads and vault, saline
and shimmering, back
to the sand and cedars.
They spook and drip, they
shake like dogs and strain at the bit
or lower their curious heads
toward the water, breathe slowly.

5.

The old white Percheron
was thirty-seven when he died
mid-winter, the ground frozen
solid as etched glass.

I could hear my father's warning:
People who name horses
after cocktails are asking
for trouble.

Memory, that smoky oil lamp
casts a warm glow against
a weathered barn wall, a track for
wagons or four-wheel drives,

leading through a valley toward a gate.

Acknowledgements

Some of these poems have previously appeared in the following publications: *dANDelion, Grain, Contemporary Verse 2, Room, The Antigonish Review, Event, Arc, The Fiddlehead, The Malahat Review,* the Parliamentary Poet Laureate's "Poem of the Week" website, *Unfurled: Collected Poetry from Northern BC Women* (Caitlin Press, 2010) and *Ice Floe: New and Selected Poems* (University of Alaska Press, 2010).

"Leaving the North" won *The Fiddlehead*'s Ralph Gustafson Poetry Prize, "Field Mice" received an honourable mention in the *Arc* Poem of the Year contest and "Driving Daytona" was selected for *The Best Canadian Poetry in English, 2010* (Tightrope Books).

I would like to thank my editor, Silas White, and my instructors and mentors through the years: in particular Rhea Tregebov for extraordinary editorial support, Keith Maillard and Miranda Pearson at UBC, and Don McKay, John Steffler and Mary Dalton at the Banff Centre for the Arts. For friendship in poetry and insights on the poems: Sheryda Warrener, Brianna Brash-Nyberg, Bren Simmers, Ria Voros, Claire Tacon, Kellee Ngan, Ben Hart, Michael John Wheeler, Michael Reynolds, Clea Roberts and all the UBC MFA class of '08 and the Banff Centre Writing Studio participants of '08.

I would like to thank the Canada Council for the Arts and the Yukon Advanced Artist Award for providing time to write.

Finally, thank you to my family and friends for all of your support, and to Justin Wallace. I love you all. This book is for you.